# PRAISING
# HIM

MARY W. JOHNSON

CROSSBOOKS'
PUBLISHING

*CrossBooks™*
*A Division of LifeWay*
*1663 Liberty Drive*
*Bloomington, IN 47403*
*www.crossbooks.com*
*Phone: 1-866-879-0502*

*First published by CrossBooks 02/20/13*

*ISBN: 978-1-4627-2529-8 (sc)*
*ISBN: 978-1-4627-2530-4 (e)*

*Printed in the United States of America*

*This book is printed on acid-free paper.*

*Any people depicted in stock imagery provided by Thinkstock are models, and such images are being used for illustrative purposes only.*

*Certain stock imagery © Thinkstock.*

# CONTENTS

Our Mother's Poetry has been published in her memory. It is our desire that this work, her legacy, will go on to bless many, as we have been blessed by her.

# ABOUT THE AUTHOR

Mary Johnson was born May 12,1914, in Wauchula, Florida. Her father was a Baptist minister, who also farmed to support the family. They moved around often in central Florida. She was the youngest child and had six brothers.

She graduated from Florida Southern College with a teaching degree in 1940. She married Bernie Johnson June 2nd later the same year. She taught first grade while raising four children: Bernice, Bill, LeAnn, and Ray. Somehow she made time to care for elderly family members in her home. Mary loved to bake and sew. She was very creative and could make and fix anything, often using her special weather-strip adhesive.

Mary taught Sunday school for many years and later taught Bible Studies. She became a Bible scholar, studying it daily. She was given God's gift of poetry at age 80. She artistically made Christmas cards with her poems inside. She wrote and made three books of poetry which she meticulously covered with wallpaper and gave them out freely to everyone.

She was a founding member of Scott Lake Baptist Church of Lakeland, Florida. Mary enjoyed reciting her poetry at the Lighthouse Mission, supported by her church. Her indelible imprint was on many, including the 150 plus that attended her ninetieth birthday party celebration at church. Her life of service was an inspiring example to all.

Mary had a lot of vitality and loved adventure. She used to say, "Go" was her middle name. She looked and acted younger than her years, and was a lot of fun to be with. She went parasailing at age 90, and a few weeks before she died went for a motorcycle ride with the "Faith Riders". Her church celebrated her life with a "Mary Johnson Appreciation Day". She was cheerful and had a smile on her face up until the very end, when she passed away of cancer in 2007, and went to heaven to meet her Savior at age 93.

Mary Johnson was 91 when this portrait was taken in 2005, for the Scott Lake Baptist Church Directory in Lakeland, Florida.

# PREFACE

I've had a lot of fun
  Using this gift God gave me,
Praising His name in verse,
  Because He loved and saved me.

If you've not trusted Jesus
  And spent time in His Word,
I hope these lines will help you
  To accept Him as your Lord.

Then love the Lord completely
  And live for Him each day
It is the way of Joy;
  There is no other way.

Wherever I've listed a scripture
  Please read every line.
God's Word's so much more important
  Than any word of mine.

# MY LIGHT

Jesus gave me a little light.
    In this dark world it will shine.
But, when Christ's glory will appear
    You'll never, never see mine.

So it's now or never for me to shine.
    Of course, it's just reflected.
It's Jesus shining all the time;
    I just redirect it.

Oh, that you might see Jesus in me
    And want this light He gave me.
This light is the joy of my life.
    And best of all, it's free.

You'll find it shining all through this book.
    And whether you're young or old,
You'll find no joy to equal this.
    He's more precious than silver or gold.

You'll find His arms are open wide
    For any who repent of sin.
Just ask Him. He will cleanse your soul;
    He'll gladly take you in.

"...I am the light of the world; he that followeth
me shall not walk in darkness, but shall have the
light of life." John 8:12

"Ye are the light of the world..." Matthew 5:14

# GOD'S GLORY

God, I thought to write of your glory,
    But that's something I cannot do.
Even Moses could not see your face,
    How can I do that for you?
Exodus 33:12-23

You put Moses in a cleft of the rock
    And covered him there with your hand;
Removed Your Hand for the afterglow,
    But Your face can't be seen by man.
Exodus 33:20

After that, the skin of his face shone,
    He covered it up with a veil.
Your glory, we cannot experience:
    Only our resurrection will avail.
Revelation 22:1-4

As to Peter, James and John, You showed
    Your glory at the transfiguration.
"They fell on their faces and were sore afraid,"
    At the terror of such visualization.
Matthew 17:1-9

For Paul on the road to Damascus,
    You had to put scales on his eyes
Before he could behold your glory,
    And be persuaded to give You his life.
Acts 9:3-18

And me! Try to write of this glory,
    How, Lord, expect that of me?
My heart just fills to overflowing.
    I'd love to do that for Thee.

But eye hath not seen nor ear heard
    Neither entered the heart of man,
Your glory at our resurrection
    And the wonderful things you have planned.
1 Corinthians 2:9

So, Jesus, I'll await that great day
    When we shall know as we're known.
That glorious resurrection morning
    When you come and claim Your own.
1 Thessalonians 4:13-18

# STEAK

When I serve a big juicy steak
    With just a touch of salt,
I don't expect anyone to say,
    "You serve up wonderful salt."

When I tell you how great God is,
    I want the world to know it.
I want them to love Him, too,
    And not to praise the poet.

If I can say a word or two
    That makes you love God better,
I will have accomplished my task.
    'Twill be worth every word and letter.

But if you start to honor me
    And praise the poems I make,
You will spoil my whole undertaking.
    That's too much salt on the steak.

# THE GIFT OF SUFFERING

We think of a gift as being something nice.
    Do you find this hard to take?
Not only given to believe on Him,
    But to suffer for His sake!
Philippians 1:29

Jesus faced untold suffering for us
    And prayed, if possible to be spared.
But the cup of suffering His Father gave Him,
    For us, He was willing to bear.
Matthew 26:39; John 18:11

We may be given fiery trials to bear
    If we live our lives for Him;
But when His glory is revealed,
    We will be glad for them.
1 Peter 4:12-13

We are clearly given a choice:
    Suffer for Him and reign with pride!
He never forces us to do anything.
    We can deny Him and be denied.
2 Timothy 2:12

The gift of suffering, more precious than gold!
    More precious than anything you can find!
Praise, Honor, Glory from Christ Himself.
    That just blows my mind!!!
1 Peter 1:6-7

# MY SALVATION

I know that I was saved
    When I was six years old.
Mother told me about Jesus.
    And I believed what she told.

I was not baptized
    Until I was nine.
But I'd trusted Jesus
    All that long, long time.

Baptized at Kathleen
    In a little creek,
I've tried to serve Jesus
    But often I am weak.

I'm so glad that God says
    In First John, One, Nine,
If I confess my sin,
    He'll forgive every time.

My worst sin is neglecting
    To do the good Lord's will.
But I just keep on trying.
    He is so precious still.

There is no way to have
    A more important day
Than that precious day,
    The day that I was saved.

# NOW'S THE TIME

It's fun to study prophecy,
    And see God's wonderful plans:
The beautiful city with golden streets,
    Prepared by Christ's dear hands.

But watch it there! For everyone
    Will not go to this place.
You must know Christ as your Lord.
    If you would see His face.

And Christian, even though heaven's fun,
    And Christ meant us to know it,
Our work now is: win the lost.
    We must care, and show it.

For those who do not choose the Lord,
    And His plan of salvation,
Will spend eternity away from God,
    In hell and degradation.

So now's the time to give your heart
    And life to serve the Lord.
When Jesus comes, 'twill be too late.
    It's clear in His dear Word.

And don't forget, when Jesus comes,
    His reward is with Him.
Your reward will all depend
    On the service that you give Him.

# ONLY CHILD

As I am getting sort of old,
    My bones begin to ache.
Sometimes I have to limp around,
    And that is hard to take.

I often wonder what I'll do;
    So much depends on me.
I just go to God and lay
    It all for Him to see.

I tell Him," You know, precious Lord,
    The job I have to do.
You know all the help I'll need;
    My strength depends on You."

He's always been right there for me
    For eighty-nine long years.
He's been so very dear to me,
    I can't hold back the tears.

Tears of joy, you know, I mean.
    He's faithful all the while.
Sometimes I think He treats me like
    I am His only child.

" The joy of the Lord is your strength."
Nehemiah 8:10

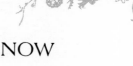

# I'M IN THE ARMY NOW

When I became a Christian,
    I joined the Lord's army.
I must stand, watch and fight
    Against the enemy.

The uniform I wear
    Must show whose side I'm on.
I must be clothed in righteousness
    And truth of God's own Son.

I must prepare for battle
    By studying His Word,
And seek the Holy Spirit
    To guide in all my work.

I mustn't stay in boot camp,
    Or go A.W.O.L.
But fight to save the lost
    From going straight to hell.

When anyone is wounded
    And fallen in the field,
I must care for them
    And see that they are healed.

I must not desert Him.
    The fields are white you see.
I can't take early retirement;
    The Lord depends on me.

I'm in the Army now!

# IF YOU WERE GOD

If you were God and you had made
    This world and all things in it,
Provided all necessities for life
    And beauty without limit,

Then have the people you had made
    Refuse to obey your laws,
Not even accept your precious Son
    Sent to amend their flaws.

What would you do?

# LIGHTHOUSE MISSION

We have a Lighthouse Mission
    That ministers to physical needs
Of people who are unfortunate,
    And need our loving deeds.

We're not prepared to do this
    In our homes; and then
They give the gospel story
    Of Jesus, the Savior of men.

I really appreciate this mission.
    They make a difference in lives.
I pray for the ones who serve there,
    And pray their good work thrives.

# TWICE MINE

A little boy, one time,
    Took just a bit of wood.
He shaped and fashioned it
    The very best he could.

He made a little boat
    And painted it bright blue.
He put a sail upon it,
    With weights and rudder, too.

He was so proud of it,
    The answer to his dream.
He took that little boat
    And sailed it on a stream.

It was a lot of fun,
    Until one fateful day,
The wind and waves came up
    And washed that boat away.

In just a day or two,
    Washed on another shore,
A man found that little boat
    And put it in his store.

He put a good price on it,
    Because it was well made.
He thought it was well worth
    The price that would be paid.

The boy went with his mother
    Down to that store one day.
He saw the boat he loved,
    And price he'd have to pay.

He made that precious boat.
    'Twas his but had been lost.
He had to have that boat,
    No matter what the cost.

He counted out his money;
    It would take all he had.
But it was worth it all;
    He wanted that boat so bad.

He ran down to that store,
    As fast as he could go,
And bought that little boat
    Because he loved it so.

He hugged it to his heart
    And said, "You are twice mine.
I made you, and I bought you.
    I loved you all the time."

Just like that little boat,
    God made us, and He bought us.
But oh! The price He paid!
    Let's make Him glad He bought us!

# FOOD

For forty years in the wilderness,
    Manna fell down every night.
Food for a million or so laid out,
    My! What a beautiful sight!

Straight from the hand of God it came
    Without their turning a hand.
All they had to do was gather it,
    On the way to the Promised Land.

Even though this "angel food" from God
    Must have tasted very good,
They complained and wanted meat to eat.
    I suppose that you and I would.

Just think of all the food you eat,
    How it varies from day to day.
We are so gloriously blessed with food,
    We can eat just any way.

The choice is ours in this wonderful land,
    Fruits, vegetables, cereals and meat.
God has provided an endless selection.
    You can have what you want to eat.

Does your heart really turn to God
    In thanks for delicious food?
For your ever changing variety?
    And the thought that it tastes so good?

# AREN'T YOU PROUD OF JESUS?

Aren't you proud of Jesus?
    Aren't you proud He loves you?
Aren't you proud he wants you
    For His very own?

Aren't you glad that someone,
    Told you of this Someone,
Who could make you someone,
    He'd want for His own?

Don't you have a brother,
    Sister or a mother,
Some friend or another,
    Who needs a Savior, too?

Whom you could tell of Jesus,
    And what He's done to please us,
So when in heaven He sees us,
    He'll be proud of you?

# NEW BODY

This body is old and bent.
   It's wrinkled and pain filled, too.
I'm glad God promised in heaven
   A body that's pure and brand new.

1 Corinthians 15:49-57
Revelation 21:4

# A MERRY HEART

Proverbs 17:22

" A merry heart doeth good like a medicine."
    But it's not a one-time dose.
Jesus is the source of joy,
    So always keep Him close.

His Word should be taken early,
    With bits of it all day long.
Take a little for meditation,
    And use it for a song.

If joy's not accomplished soon,
    You may have to take it double.
It works best in concentrated form,
    To keep you out of trouble.

His Word's been known to change a life,
    From darkness into light,
Lifting desires from things of earth,
    To heaven's lofty heights.

If you need some extra pep
    And you want a merry heart,
Jesus has the medicine you need,
    And now's the time to start.

It's all wrapped up in a package,
    Just waiting for your call:
Old Testament and New Testament,
    Be sure to use it all.

# TO THE ATHEIST

If you think there is no God,
    There is.
If you think there is no hell,
    There is.
If you think He wants to send you there,
    He doesn't.
God showed His power
    In creation.
For your pleasure He made
    All things beautiful.
When we messed up, God
    Sent His Son.
Jesus' death for your sins provides
    Heaven.
He offers it for free to those who
    Believe.
Accept it or die for your own sins
    In hell.
It's your choice. Accept it or
    Leave it.
Hell is forever, No chance
    After death.
When you are burning in
    Hell,
Don't say I didn't
    Warn you.
It can be different.
    Choose Jesus.
In choosing Jesus, you choose heaven.
    Do it.

# BEING BORN AGAIN

I know you've heard; do you understand
    What it means to be born again?
You can be born into the family of God,
    As you live in the family of men.

You first must know who Jesus is:
    Eternal God, came to live as man,
With sinless blood to cleanse our sins,
    One with the Father e'er the world began.

It is a mystery, what really takes place.
    It involves a change of your heart.
Jesus becomes the Lord of your life.
    That's where it all must start.

To make Him Lord, you have to know
    The things that He commands.
This you must learn through Bible study,
    To find what His Law demands.

The wonderful part about being born again,
    Is the Holy Spirit He provides,
To take the place of our sinful spirit,
    He comes in your heart and abides.

Though the Holy Spirit is always there,
    Satan never leaves you alone.
When born again, you'll constantly try
    To keep Jesus on the throne.

It's so exciting, being a child of God,
    And knowing we'll see Him some day,
And all the other precious promises.
    No power can take away!

    Hallelujah!

# A NEW CREATION

God looked down at this world He created,
 And, "behold, it was very good."
There's no way we could improve on it.
 Just try if you think you could.
Genesis 1:31

God has in mind a new creation;
 But He won't tell us much about it,
But if He says it's going to be good,
 I have no reason to doubt it.
2 Peter 3:9-13; Revelation 21

There's one thing sure: I want to go there,
 And He has shown us the way.
He's given us His very own WORD.
 Just read it and accept Him today.
John 14:6

He said that you can go there, too.
 For whosoever believes on him,
Will have eternal life with Him,
 And will never be condemned.
John 3:16, 36

# CHRIST AROSE! SO WHAT?

Now that we've all praised the Lord,
  On His glorious Resurrection Day,
What are we going to do about it?
  Treat it as just any other day?

Are we going to just keep going along
  Our non-caring merry way?
And not tell a soul what Jesus did
  By rising on that special day?

Are we not going to spread the good news
  That His promises do come true?
Just as He said He would rise again,
  His sacrifice can avail for you.

What if Mary, the one who first saw Him,
  And the apostles to whom He appeared,
And all who experienced His resurrection,
  Had kept it to themselves and not shared?

You and I would all perish,
  Eternally separated from the Lord,
If those people back then had kept silent,
  And not given their lives to spread the word.

So what are we going to do?
  Just let the world go to hell?
Because we didn't care enough
  To take a little time to tell?

# THANK YOU FOR THE DARKNESS

Acts 26:18; 1 Peter 2:9

If our way was all planned out,
    Each step was written down,
We'd never know how much we need
    To have the Lord around.

If our path was plain as day,
    No question about the right,
We'd never go to God above
    To seek the heavenly light.

If we could buy our way to heaven,
    Out of the fix we're in,
We'd never seek the Lamb of God,
    Who cleanses us from sin.

So thank You for the darkness,
    So we will seek Your light.
And thank You for the Holy Spirit,
    Who guides us in the right.

Thank you for the Bible,
    That makes our way so plain.
And thanks, again, for Jesus,
    Who bore our awful pain.

If Jesus had not died for us,
    We'd never praise the Son.
And if we never suffer for Him,
    We'll never hear, "Well done."

# HOW MUCH DO YOU LOVE HIM?

Would you climb a tree
    To get a peek at Jesus?
I'm sure that there is someone
    Who would surely tease us.
Luke 19:1-10

Would you go next door,
    Or just across the street,
To tell the blessed story
    Of Christ, whom they should meet?
Acts 1:8

Or are you ashamed
    Of Jesus and His Word?
Or are you too involved
    With the things of this world?
Mark 8:38; Matthew 22:4-5

Do you use more money,
    To try to win the lottery,
Than you give to Jesus,
    Who has untold treasures laid up for thee?
1 Corinthians 2:9

This verse is for those who love Him!
Just how much DO you love Him?
John 14:24

# ISN'T THAT JUST LIKE JESUS?

When man had messed up and sinned and died,
Only a God of mercy and love
Could have thought of resurrection,
To live with Him in glory above!

# HIS TIME HAD COME

There's no way Jesus could die,
  Until His work was done.
Try as they did at Nazareth,
  To kill the Holy One.
Luke 4:16-30

As Jesus taught in the temple,
  They showed wrath toward the Son.
They took up stones to stone Him,
  But He passed through the midst and was gone.
John 8:57-59

When the Pharisees sent to take Him,
  Nothing could be done.
He confounded them with His speech.
  No one could take Him! Not one!
John 7:32, 44-46

Even Satan himself had tried it.
  He thought he would have some fun.
He told Christ to cast himself down,
  But his dirty game was not won.
Matthew 4:5-7

The soldiers could not even take Him,
  Though His time had really come.
They went backward and fell to the ground!
  With no power over the Blessed Son.
John 18:3-6

He then just gave Himself to them.
  The Father's will must be done.
Praise You, Jesus, our precious Savior.
  Through You, our victory is won.
1 John 5:1-4

# FINISHED?

When Jesus said, "It is finished," on the cross,
    The sacrifice had been made.
The way for eternal life was opened.
    The price in full had been paid.
John 19:30

But He had said there was one thing more,
    That He was sent to do.
He had to preach deliverance to captives.
    This must be accomplished, too.
Luke 4:18

The captives were held in the heart of the earth,
    In a place called paradise,
Held there until their souls were redeemed,
    And Jesus from death would arise.
Matthew 12:40; Luke 23:43
1 Peter 3:18-19; Luke 16:19-31

This is explained a lot more fully
    In Ephesians 4, 8 through 10.
Jesus had to deliver those captives,
    Held in paradise up until then.

Paul let us in on the secret:
    Paradise is no longer down.
This man "was caught up into paradise."
    Jesus took it there, I have found.
2 Corinthians 12:3-4

So as He builds his church, the gates of hell
    (Hades) do "not prevail against it."
Matthew 16:18

# KIN FOLKS

If you've been born again,
　　I, too, have been made free.
Since God's our heavenly Father,
　　You are kin to me.

I am your older sister,
　　For I love your Savior, too.
With all your life before you,
　　No telling what you can do.

A child resembles his parents.
　　As a child of God, we must, too.
Not physical—we never saw Jesus—
　　But like Him in things that we do.

"But that's too hard," you may say.
　　Right! But don't gripe and groan.
He gave the Holy Spirit,
　　So you never have to work alone.

Each day your life is a witness
　　Of what you are today.
I'm praying your life and words
　　Will help show others the way.

There was joy in the presence of angels
　　When you repented of sin.
You'll make them rejoice again
　　When you bring someone to Him.
Luke 15:10

# WOULD YOU?

Would you, a mighty man of valor,
　　Suffering with leprosy,
Dip seven times in the Jordan,
　　To let others God's power see?
　　　　Naaman did.
　　　　2 Kings 5:1-14

Would you suffer blindness from birth
　　Till you were a man, full grown,
That the works of God be manifest,
　　And the power of Jesus be known?
　　　　The man in John 9 did.
　　　　John 9:1-38

Would you put Jesus ahead of food,
　　And sit at Jesus' feet to learn of Him,
With sister trying to pull you away
　　To fix a meal for them?
　　　　Mary did.
　　　　Luke 10:38-42

Would you lie in the grave for days,
　　Awaiting the shining hour,
When Jesus would say "Lazarus come forth!"
　　To prove His resurrection power?
　　　　Lazarus did.
　　　　John 11:34-44

Would you take your family to church,
　　And talk of the Savior at home,
And present the gospel story,
　　In a personal way to each one?
　　　　My parents did.

# WILL YOU?

Acts 9:1-10

If you were Ananias,
    And you had heard of Paul,
How he persecuted Christians,
    But you had heard God's call,

You felt your life in danger.
    Yet Jesus said 'twas alright.
Paul needed you to come,
    That he might receive his sight.

God chose Ananias,
    To minister unto Paul,
Not just have sight restored,
    But receive the Holy Spirit and all.
                Would you go?

John 20:21
Jesus has chosen you,
    To tell the world of Him.
Will you heed His call?
    Will you be true to them?
                Will you go?

Ananias answered God's call.
    Paul still ministers the Word to us.
If you obey and go,
    Only God knows the results.
                Will you go?

# SHE HAD NO BIBLE

I bought a Bible for a lady.
　　She promised to read it through.
Months later she hadn't even started.
　　She had other things to do.

I bought a Bible for another lady.
　　I often hear her say
How much she enjoys God's Word,
　　As she reads it every day.

Which Bible do you think I was glad I bought?
　　'Twas a simple act of love.
Which life do you think Christ was glad He bought
　　With His own precious blood?

# STILL WRAPPED TOGETHER

John 11:43-44; John 20:6-7


Wouldn't you love to have seen Peter,
    Run to the tomb and go in,
See all those grave clothes still wrapped together,
    Showing where Jesus had been.

Undisturbed by his resurrection,
    Lazarus, they had to "loose and let go."
Jesus came right through those wrappings.
    He had that power, you know.

# IN LOVE WITH JESUS

Are you in love with Jesus?
    Do you hold Him most dear?
Does He consume your every thought?
    Do you feel His presence near?

He created us and loved us.
    But love must be returned.
Have you ever loved someone,
    And had the pure love spurned?

Imagine the creator of all things
    Squandering His love on you,
And then having that love rejected.
    What should our Savior do?

He's not just given us this great world,
    But paid for our life of sin,
And given us all kinds of promises
    Of life in heaven with Him.

Just think! This powerful creator,
    And sustainer of all things,
Showering all His love on us!
    This Lord of Lords and King of kings!

Who on earth could reject this love?
    It's beyond my comprehension.
Fall in love with Jesus now!
    He's worth all your love and attention.

# MANY CHOICES

We think of angels as perfect,
    Doing the Father's will,
Ministering to the saved ones,
    The scripture, to fulfill.
Hebrews 1:13-14

But some of the angels sinned,
    And had to be put away.
They're held in chains of darkness,
    Awaiting the judgment day.
2 Peter 2:4; Jude 6

Adam and Eve were told
    Not to eat of one special tree.
But eat of that tree they did,
    And death passed to you and me.
Romans 5:12

Noah lived six hundred years,
    And he had never seen rain.
It took faith to build that ark,
    So his family could remain.
Genesis 2:5-6; Hebrews 11:7

He preached but he had no takers.
    God gave them one hundred twenty years.
The world suffered death by the flood.
    Listening would have saved death and tears.
Genesis 6:3; 2 Peter 2:5

Sodom was filled with homosexuals;
    Even tried to use angels as men.
When the fire of judgment fell,
    No one could save them then.
Genesis 19:1-28

Why am I writing all this?
    I'll tell you the reason why.
God warned you and me of sin.
    "The soul that sinneth, it shall die."
Ezekiel 18:4,20

But death's not the end of all things.
    There's coming a judgment day.
Saved and lost will be resurrected,
    Avoid it as hard as you may.
John 5:24-29

There's wonderful news about Jesus,
    Who made man for His own,
Set aside His glory for awhile,
    And came for sin to atone.
Hebrews 1:1-3; 2:9-10

Salvation truly is a free gift.
    But to be yours, it must be received.
It's your life for His is the deal.
    Give Him your life when you've believed.
Romans 12:1-2

Life on this earth is uncertain,
    And Jesus may come any day.
Unless you are ready to meet Him,
    There just is no other way.
Acts 4:12

It is your choice, my friend.
    The choice is for heaven or hell.
Be sure your faith is in Jesus.
    So with you, all shall be well.
Revelation 20:11-15

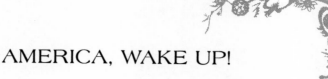

# AMERICA, WAKE UP!

What would you do if you were God,
    To a nation who turned Him down,
Put Him out of schools and government,
    And didn't want Him around?

All that He would have to do,
    Is turn us loose one minute.
This whole universe would collapse,
    The world and all things in it.

For it is God's great power and strength,
    Not only that made it all,
But holds it all complete together.
    Without Him all would fall.

Just look what He's done to Israel.
    He's turned His back on them.
Imagine what he'll do to America
    If we don't turn back to Him.

When Israel recognizes their King,
    He's promised to restore them.
We have no such promises.
    It's now or never to adore Him!

**AMERICA, WAKE UP!**

# NEED RAIN?

Have you ever prayed for rain?
    I have, then looked at myself.
Why should God send me rain,
    When I'd put God on the shelf?

I've spent my time on things I want,
    And things that benefit me,
Instead of spending time with God,
    And asking Him what He'd have me be.

If I really do love God,
    I'll listen to His Word.
I'll hear with my heart, His message,
    And act on what I have heard.

He says doing things for others,
    Is the way to do things for Him.
I can show my love for Jesus,
    By loving and helping them.

So, dear Lord, just open my eyes,
    To things you would have me do.
I must obey your commands,
    If I want to ask things from you.

# SWEET BAY

When just a kid, beyond our house
    There was a lovely wood.
I loved that place and would go there
    Every time I could.

I'd take a twig to make a doll.
    (I guess I was a mess.)
I'd take a bay leaf, wrap it 'round,
    And there! I had a dress.

On Sundays Mother took us there
    And stories would begin.
It thrilled my heart to know Christ died
    To take away our sin.

I loved the trees and flowers there;
    But bay trees I loved best.
The perfume of those sweet bay blossoms
    Stood out from all the rest.

For eighty years, I longed to smell
    That sweet fragrance again.
Out of reach, along highways,
    I'd see those blossoms. And then!

Pat planted one beside the lake
    For all of us to see.
Who should she give her first blossom to?
    You guessed it! It was ME!

Thank you Pat, I love you,
    For giving that to me,
And thank you, Jesus; I love you,
    For making them so sweet.

# CHURCH ATTIRE

When you come to church,
　　Christ is looking at you.
Are you properly dressed?
　　Or like the world would do?

Some shorts and short skirts,
　　Just make my face turn red.
I'm afraid that Jesus
　　Has to turn his head.

You may call me "old fogie".
　　If so, I do not care,
For I am sure that Jesus
　　Cares about what you wear.

Pardon me, my dear ones,
　　If I stepped on your toes.
But really, girls, you know,
　　Christ cares about your clothes.

# THE CHRISTMAS CARD

This special Christmas card
    Shocked and touched me so!
Just a little footprint
    On a sheet, white as snow.

I wanted to kiss it
    And hold it close
As if those had been
    My Savior's toes.

As if His foot
    Had touched that sheet
And then pulled away
    And gone to sleep.

It felt like He
    Had really been there.
I had to turn
    And kneel in prayer,

And thank Him once more
    For bringing to earth
Such heavenly love
    In His human birth.

And then I opened it;
    And what did I see?
That nail-pierced hand
    Reaching out to me.

That shock was more
    Than I could bear,
My Savior's hand
    Still bleeding there.

It brought it all back,
    That precious story,
Even though now
    He's up in glory.

I still had to cry
    And thank Him again
For bringing such love
    To us wicked men.

# WHY ALL THE LIGHTS AT CHRISTMAS?

Jesus said:
"I am the light of the world."
John 8:12

He also said:
"Ye are the light of the world."
Matthew 5:14

As the moon faithfully reflects
    The light of the SUN,

May we just as faithfully reflect
    The light of the SON.

Christmas lights reminds us of the
    Light Jesus brought to man.

# ENOUGH

When I was born the first time,
    Eighty-nine years ago,
My food was only milk,
    But then I had to grow.

I, very soon, needed meat,
    Vegetables and fruits and stuff.
I ate all kinds of food;
    I couldn't get enough.

When I was born again,
    Milk of the word was fine.
Milk will give you a good start,
    But don't stay there all the time.

When I got down to study,
    Deep into God's precious word,
I couldn't get enough;
    My whole being was stirred.

You, too, can know the thrill
    Of thinking God's thoughts after Him.
You'll never get enough;
    You'll always find new gems!

Here's a little surprise package.
    God doesn't have enough yet.
Read Malachi 3:16 and 17.
    You'll want to be His jewel, I bet.

# JESUS' SWEETHEART

If we're to be the bride
    Of Christ some day, somehow,
Then it just stands to reason,
    That we're his sweetheart now.
Revelation 21:2,9; Ephesians 5:21-33

It really isn't hard
    To figure that all out.
Just look at all the blessings
    And gifts He gives us now.
James 1:17

It's just as if He's courting us
    To be his heavenly spouse.
Someday we'll gladly wed
    And in His presence bow.
Romans 14:11

He's already "popped the question".
    What is your answer now?
Have you said, "Yes", to Jesus?
    Or do you now know how?
Revelation 22:17

If you'll read all these scriptures
    They will tell you how
To be espoused to Jesus
    And with His riches endowed.

| | |
|---|---|
| Romans 3:23 | John 3:36 |
| Romans6:23 | Ephesians 2:8-9 |
| Romans 5:8 | Luke 12:32 |
| John 3:16-17 | 1 Corinthians 2:9 |

WOW!

# THAT MARY

Oh, that I had been that Mary
    God chose to bear His Son!
That I could have held in my arms
    That precious Holy One!

How I would have rejoiced,
    When shepherds came that night,
And told of the message from angels,
    And glory of that heavenly light,

How glorious would have been that moment
    That Simeon took my child,
And told the world my secret,
    I'd carried all the while:

That my child would bring salvation,
    For He was God's own Son.
And Anna, that little old lady,
    Confirmed that He was the One.

How my heart would have thrilled each day,
    Seeing Him grow and be so wise,
As the Spirit filled his being,
    And showed grace in all our eyes.

I am sure that that Mary's heart
    Was somewhat eased that third day,
When her precious Son arose,
    And proved He was The Way.

But her heart could never erase
    The horror of what her son went through,
Nor can I ever recall it,
    Without going all to pieces, too.

If I had been that Mary,
    And seen all His miracles and power,
I'm sure I could not have understood
    How Satan could have ruled that hour,

And crucified my precious Jesus,
    And desecrated His body so,
Though Simeon had told me in the temple,
    "A sword should pierce through my soul, also."

I wasn't chosen to be that Mary.
    He had other plans for me.
But my heart just breaks to pieces
    When I think of His agony.

I don't know how it could hurt more,
    Or my heart break more for one,
Had I been chosen to be that Mary,
    And Jesus were my very own Son.

# A NEW COMMANDMENT

John 13:34

Jesus commanded us to love one another.
He called this commandment new.
What was new about loving one another?
He added, "as I have loved you."

# MUSTARD SEED FAITH

Luke 17:6

Did you read this verse?
 What did it say to you?
Do you have mustard seed faith?
 What would God have you do?

What kind of faith is this,
 That a mustard seed has "got"?
In the first place it doesn't worry
 Whether it has faith or not.

It just puts down its roots,
 Sometimes in a place that's new,
And starts doing the job
 God created it to do.

It doesn't worry if the soil
 Will supply nutrients where it fell,
Or whether the rain, or someone,
 Will water it real well.

It doesn't get impatient
 For what it does to show.
It just looks up to God and
 Trusts Him to make it grow.

Looking back at the scripture verse,
 I don't want to remove a tree.
I just want to touch hearts
 And turn them, Lord, to thee.

# I LOVE CHRISTMAS

I love the trees at Christmas
    But it really saddens me,
As I remember the fact
    That Jesus died on a tree.

I love the lights at Christmas
    Around the tree all curled.
They make me think of Jesus
    The light of this dark world.

As branches bear those lights,
    Upon that Christmas tree,
I must remember to bear
    The light Christ gave to me.

I love to see a star,
    Atop those Christmas trees,
For Christ, our Morning Star,
    Does everything to please.

I love the carols at Christmas
    About our Savior King.
I love to see the joy
    As little children sing.

I love the presents at Christmas
    With wrappings and ribbons and fuss,
But no gift can top the one
    Christ gave—Himself—for us.

# MAKE GOD HAPPY

What makes a mother happy?
    What makes a father proud?
Having a child who loves you,
    And wants to be around.

It's hard to believe, but it's true,
    That our heavenly Father up there,
Is happy when we spend time
    With Him in His Word and prayer.

We expect our children to come,
    And spend the holidays with us.
Christmas is the Lord's birthday.
    Spending time with Him is a must.

And what about family and friends?
    We give Christmas gifts to them.
Remember it's Christ's birthday.
    What gift will you give to Him?

Help make this Christmas happy
    For the one whose birthday we share.
Love Him with all your heart.
    And show the Lord that you care.

The gift that will make Him happiest
    And will also bring joy to you,
Is to bring a lost soul to Jesus
    And have him love Jesus, too.

# HE HUMBLED HIMSELF

He Humbled Himself and Became a Man
    Because, as God, He Could Not Die.

Not just humbled to become a man,
    But He suffered that which no other can.
The physical suffering was beyond compare.
    But the spotless lamb bore the sins of man.

# YOUR CHOICE

Whether or not you believe,
    Jesus died for you.
He died, not just for believers,
    But for the whole world, too.
If you do not believe me,
    Read First John 2, verse 2.

If you refuse Him now,
    Eternity in hell you'll receive,
Not for your sins—they've been paid for—
    But because you would not believe.
John 3:36, Jesus said it,
    And Jesus would not deceive.

So with the Savior in glory
    Or with Satan—which do you choose?
You alone make the choice.
    It's entirely up to you.
But friend, just think about it.
    Heaven is too good to lose.

# PRAISE YOU, JESUS!

No hospital bed with sterile sheets,
    No room for them in the inn,
As Mary and Joseph sought refuge,
    Not even the comfort of kin.

No nurse to attend Mary's labor
    That holy first Christmas morn.
No doctor to make the delivery
    When the Great Physician was born.

'Twas not a fancy cradle
    In which the Christ Child lay,
But just a lowly manger
    On a soft bed of hay.

We love you, precious Jesus,
    For wanting us for your own,
For coming and suffering and dying
    To provide our eternal home.

Praise Him with Me!

# LITTLE LAMB

I'd love to have been a lamb,
    In the stable that Holy night,
When Jesus Christ came down
    To shed His heavenly Light.

# STICK OUT

A small boy asked his dad
    How tall Jesus was.
His dad said, "six feet tall."
    Then after a short pause,

The boy said, "If He's six feet,
    And I am four—about-
If Jesus is inside of me,
    Then Jesus must stick out."

I hope I never get too big,
    Or rich or tall or stout,
Or think of other things too much
    To let my Lord stick out.

# BE HAPPY ANYWAY

Has someone tried to slight you?
    Or said things hard to bear?
Don't let it get you down.
    Just breathe their name in prayer.

Be happy anyway, my dear,
    No matter what they've done.
It probably will confound them,
    And it's a lot more fun.

# CHOOSE JESUS

When Christmas is all over,
    And Baby Jesus out of mind,
Don't ever forget the One
    The Wise Men had to find.

He'd always been divine,
    That perfect Holy One.
When He was born of Mary.
    He became God's Son.

He endured rejection,
    And death by cruel men,
All to pay the price
    For all our wretched sin.

He took on human flesh,
    So that He could die.
And that stops eternal death
    For sinners such as I.

If He could not have risen
    From death as He had said,
We'd have no assurance
    We'd rise from the dead.

But He did rise again,
    Just like He said, and then,
Made us the precious promise:
    We, too, will rise again.

Yes, we will rise again;
    And our choice now will tell:
Eternity in heaven,
    Or in a place called hell.

You have the choice to make.
    It's your life for His own.
Live for Him here on earth
    And heaven will be your home.

If you refuse His offer,
    There's only one place more.
It's too horrible to mention,
    What you will have in store.

Choose Jesus!!!

# WHO PAYS?

Does the maker of the universe
Care for the likes of me and you?
1 Timothy 1:15

The thought of it just boggles my mind.
It seems impossible but it's true.
John 3:16

He made the law of sin and death.
And that law must be obeyed.
Ezekiel 18:4,20

Our sin requires the death penalty.
By Christ's death our sin-debt is paid.
Romans 5:8

# GIVING TO GOD

You've heard of the tithe before,
    And that's what the law demands,
But you say, "We are free
    From the law and its commands".

Say, tell me, precious one,
    Are you glad to be free?
Would you be under the law?
    Really? That is not for me!

I'd surely not give less,
    Since I have been made free,
Than was required by law,
    Under which they had to be.

I'm so glad I am free.
    I want to show my love.
I give, not under the law,
    Under which they had to be.

I'm so glad I am free.
    I want to show my love.
I give, not under the law,
    But love for God above.

What will you give to God,
    Who made you free from sin,
Made you a home in heaven,
    And bade you enter in?

"For God so loved He gave",
    And if I love 'twill show.
I want to give and give,
    To the one who loves me so.

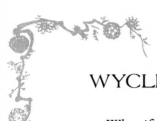

# WYCLIFFE TRANSLATORS

What if you lived far away?
　　Maybe Asia or Borneo.
And Christ died for your sins, too,
　　But you just didn't know.

What if you'd not even seen
　　The Bible or heard God's word?
Your language was not written down,
　　But only just been heard.

Tell me how you'd ever know
　　That Jesus cared for you,
And died upon that cruel cross,
　　To pay for your sins, too.

You know there are ones who give
　　Their lives to meet such needs.
Wycliffe Translators are the ones
　　That go wherever God leads.

They have to learn the language,
　　Then have to write it down.
Then comes the very tedious part:
　　Translating into what they've found.

Even so, it takes many years.
　　It's harder than you've heard.
Then the natives have to learn to read,
　　To enjoy God's Holy Word.


God Bless You, Wycliffe Translators!

# THE REAL THING

I told my children early,
    About Jesus and His love,
About his dying to save us,
    And plans for heaven above.

I told them how mothers brought children,
    To meet the Savior King.
It would have been fun if my children
    Could have met "the real thing"!

For that we'll wait awhile.
    When they meet "the real thing",
He'll be in all His glory.
    'Twill be the really "real thing"!

# IDLE WORDS

Matthew 12:36

This little verse worries me,
    But I guess, not very much.
Not enough to make me stop,
    In fun, making jokes and such.

It says in the day of judgment,
    Men shall give account
Of every idle word they speak!
    I have a vast amount.

I'm not just sure what this verse means.
    I really don't think Christ minds
About words spoken in clean fun;
    Better cause laughs than whines.

# "WE PREACH CHRIST CRUCIFIED"

1 Corinthians 1:23

Ever wonder why Paul said,
 "We preach Christ crucified"?
And not Christ risen from the dead?
 Or ascended, or glorified?

The crucifixion's what paid our sin debt,
 The "Lamb" as our sacrifice.
The resurrection and ascension proved
 That payment would suffice.

So thank you, Jesus, for dying,
 And paying our debt of sin.
And thank you for your promise
 That you're coming back again.

# IN JESUS' NAME

Did anyone ever write a check
    And sign your name to it?
Yet we pray God, "in Jesus' name",
    And expect the Lord to do it.

Jesus didn't pray in his own name,
    'please take this cup away."
He prayed, "Not my will but Thine be done."
    And God's will was done that day.

What if He'd said, "I'll not take their sin.
    I just cannot go through it?
It's entirely too much to ask of me.
    They will just have to do it?"

The grief that we would have to bear
    Is just too much to tell.
All that we could look forward to
    Would be eternity in hell.

But praise the Lord, Christ took my sin.
    And He took your sin, too.
Accept His free gift of salvation.
    That's all you have to do.

Of course, it's your life for His life.
    Since He has given His all.
We live our lives to honor him,
    Who ransomed us from the fall.

# THE CRUCIFIXION

John 13-17

These chapters take place in the upper room.
    They're the "last words" to ones He loved so.
They would supply much assurance
    To them since Jesus had to go.

These disciples would be sorely tested,
    Not just then but for years as they preach.
They also thrill us now, today,
    The wonderful things that they teach.

Matthew 26,27; Mark 14,15
Luke 22,23; John 18,19

Then as He agonized there in the garden,
    The disciples could not help but sleep.
When the soldiers took Him, they fled.
    No one for His capture to weep.

To Annas, to Caiaphas, to Pilate,
    To Herod, and then back again.
No one but wicked accusers,
    At the trial of the Savior of men.

No one to plead His case,
    As they bound Him and spit in His face.
Though Pilate found no fault in Him,
    He scourged Him and released Barabbas in his place.

No nurse to apply soothing ointment
    To the cruel thorn wounds on His head.
No one to stop the angry mob
    Until the death sentence was read.

No advocate when they cried, "Crucify Him."
    He even had to carry His own cross,
Until Simon bore it after Him.
    No one to cry, "Please, please stop!"

No doctor to bind up those cruel nail wounds.
    John and His mother hear Him sigh.
This was decreed from the beginning;
    He just had to hang there and die.

No soft-pillowed coffin for His body;
    Just a cold hard tomb carved in rock,
Laid there by Joseph and Nicodemus.
    A great stone to the door formed a lock.

Chief priests sealed the tomb and set a watch,
    Thinking they could keep Jesus in.
The angels in heaven must have laughed
    At their thinking He could be held by men.

Isaiah 53:4-5; 1 Peter 2:24

The greatness in this story for us
    Is that He bore your and my sin.
He died the death meant for us
    To open heaven and let us in.

Such love I just cannot fathom.
    I can only live my life for Him,
And tell this precious sweet story
    To the world, for it's meant for them.

# MORE ABOUT JESUS

If you were in a ship,
    And wind and waves came up,
And seemed about to swallow
    That ship in one great gulp,

Then "Peace, be still," From Jesus,
    Made every wave lie still,
The mighty wind calm down,
    Obeying the Master's will,
Mark 4:35-41

Wouldn't you also exclaim
    "what manner of man is this?"
And be obedient, like those waves,
    And become a servant of His?
Matthew 8:23-27

What if you saw a man,
    Who was often on your mind,
Because you knew for certain
    That he had been born blind.

And then this man could see
    Because Jesus made him well.
You'd want to know more about Jesus,
    All that any could tell.
John 9:1-38

What if, one day, you were going along
    And a dead man was carried out.
Jesus touched his bed and that man
    Came to life and rose up? You would shout!
Luke 7:11-15

Another day He healed ten lepers.
　　Only one came back and praised.
To see one that had such power,
　　I'm sure that you'd be amazed.
Luke 17:11-19

Forty years, two million Israelites
　　Were fed daily manna by Him.
When five thousand men were hungry,
　　Do you wonder that He could feed them?
Exodus 16:35; John 6:5-14

But there is food more important,
　　The food that makes the soul blessed.
God's library has sixty-six books.
　　That's soul-food at its very best.
Matthew 4:4

What if you saw this Jesus,
　　Hated and beaten and spit on,
And hung on that wretched cross,
　　Until you could tell every bone.
Psalm 22:14-18

Then hear him say, "Father forgive them.
　　They know not what they do."
Wouldn't you love Him forever?
　　And be his disciple, too?
Luke 23:34

Just see Him hang there and die
　　And see Him rise from the dead,
You'd want to know all about Him.
　　It's all there, just waiting to be read.

The Bible

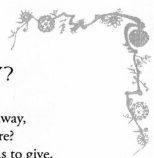

# DRIFTED AWAY?

Are you a Christian who's drifted away,
    And don't go to church anymore?
You accept all the blessings God has to give,
    But church to you is a bore!

Have you neglected your Christian friends?
    Your knowledge of the Bible is dim.
Have you forgotten the joy you once had
    In a Sunday School class with them?

Do you use your talents all for yourself,
    When they could be used for the Lord?
Is your time filled up with all kinds of things?
    And you spend no time in His Word?

God used His wonderful unsearchable mind,
    To plan and create this land.
He put in this world all things we need.
    Don't you just love all he planned?

His laws are perfect if they are kept,
    But first we must learn to obey.
Adam brought death by rebelling,
    And we suffer death still today.

"The soul that sinneth it shall die,"
    Is one law I remember.
He also made another law:
    The law of the kinsman redeemer.

To bear our sins and redeem us,
    He had to be one of our kin.
That is why our Lord came down
    And lived in a body as men.

Then he showed the most awesome love
    That anyone can think of today.
He suffered horrible death on the cross
    To take all our sins away.

My whole being dissolves into tears
    At the thought that He did this for me.
He died for you, too, and if you've believed,
    He's redeemed you from sin and you're free.

It's your life for His; He gave all for you.
    Don't throw your whole life away.
Consider all the Lord's done for you
    And give Him back your life today.

# I'M HIS

I'm having a happy day
    No matter what day it is,
For Jesus, the Savior is mine.
    And you know what? I'm His!

# WHEN I GET TO HEAVEN

When I get to heaven,
    And I will some day!
In heaven—oh dear!
    What will I say?

First, why am I Here?
    I'm so glad I am.
All praises go
    To the precious Lamb.

One look at Jesus,
    I'll fall on my face,
And thank Him forever
    For His precious grace.

When I catch my breath,
    From the glory of His being,
I'll get off my face
    And enjoy what I'm seeing.

I'll thank Christ again
    For going to earth,
Providing for us
    That precious new birth.

And letting us be called
    His brother or His sister,
If we were obedient
    And not just a listener.

I'll thank Him for His love,
    In spite of our sin,
And thank Him for letting
    Us children come in.

I knew heaven was great.
    He told us the story.
But how, down on earth,
    Could we understand glory?

I'll fall on my face
    Again and give praise,
When I see the Father,
    The Ancient of Days.

I'd not neglect
    To praise the Spirit,
Who opened the Word
    And gave faith to hear it.

When I had the strength,
    I'd join angels and sing
Blessing and honor
    And praise to the King.

I really can't know
    About all this stuff.
Just being with Jesus
    Will be quite enough.

# VALENTINE DEVOTION 2003

Revelation 19:7-8; Isaiah 64:6; 2 Corinthians 5:21

Can you remember your first love?
How the thought of him thrilled you!
And when he stopped to speak to you,
You treasured even a word or two.

Guys, remember that little cute thing
Who first stole your heart away.
And when she slipped a note to you,
I bet you remember today.

Maybe that first love didn't last,
But now you have found the right one,
One you promised to love and cherish,
Through life, and then up above.

And as this love began to grow,
You wanted your time together.
When separated even a short while,
You anxiously awaited a letter.

This reminiscing's to make us think
Of our most precious love,
The one who loved us all so much,
He left His throne up above.

Worse than leprosy, cancer or AIDS,
We had the blight of sin,
The curse that barred us all from heaven.
No way could we enter in.

That precious Jesus showed His love,
    By laying down His life.
He suffered the agony of the cross,
    To cleanse for himself a wife.

I talked about treasuring each word
    Your loved one wrote to you.
Jesus sent you endless letters.
    Read them. They're always new.

If you're really in love with Jesus,
    You'll treasure every word.
The Bible will mean more to you
    Than anything you've seen or heard.

You'll spend time not lightly reading,
    But studying the deep things of God.
You'll want to know His precious promises,
    And understand His rod.

When the Bridegroom's shout rings out,
    You'll meet Him in the air,
Dressed in His righteousness alone,
    To ever be with Him there.

He's not just given us this great earth,
    But paid for our life of sin,
And given us all kinds of promises,
    Of life in heaven with Him.

# WITH HIM

2 Timothy 2:12


If we suffer for Him,
   We shall reign with Him.
Some folk like to reign.
   I'm not one of them.

But
We're the bride of Christ.
   The bride's next to His heart.
Jesus does the "reigning".
   We're the "with Him" part.

# THE TRINITY

Though some complain that "trinity"
    Is not found in the Bible,
But it's the heart of scripture,
    And its use is reliable.

We're told there is but one God,
    And that His name is One,
Even though we know our God
    As Father, Spirit and Son.

God said, "Let us make man
    After our own image."
The plural US and OUR
    Were used at the beginning.

We, too, are made a "trinity,"
    Body, soul and spirit
And we are Just as much one
    As Father, Son and Spirit.
1 Thessalonians 5:23

Christ said, "I'm in the Father
    And the Father is in me".
But Father, Son and Spirit,
    Were separated at Calvary.

At death we, too, separate.
　　Our spirit goes to God,
Though our body may rest,
　　Beneath this earthly sod.

Christ's body did not remain
　　Separated from God. Oh, Hear it!
But was resurrected,
　　Joining Father and the Spirit.

Do you know what He promised
　　If we believe on His name?
Though we may be in the grave,
　　We'll be resurrected just the same.

We'll hear that great trump of God.
　　The shout of Christ will be heard.
We'll join Him in the air,
　　And we'll ever be with the Lord!

# READ ON

If you are not a Christian,
    Read Romans 3:23
You'll not go to heaven.
    You're lost as you can be.
Read On.

But I have news for you:
    That does not have to be.
Jesus made a way.
Read: Romans 6:23
Read On

A father loves his son,
    If you know what I mean,
But God gave His Son for us.
Read : John 3:16
Read On.

You don't have to be good.
    You don't have to wait.
Christ came to save sinners.
Read Romans 5, verse 8.
Read On.

If you want to be saved,
    You must repent of sin.
For what you have to do,
    Read Romans 10:9 and 10.
Read On.

When He saves you, you will love Him.
    There's one good way to show it.
Read John 14, verse 15.
    This will make Jesus know it.
Read On.

For your spiritual life to grow,
    And to really enjoy the Lord,
Read Matthew 4, verse 4,
    And immerse yourself in His Word.
Read On.

Don't try to pay for salvation.
    Read Ephesians 2:8 through 10.
When you have faith to believe
    You are saved and "works" start then.
Read On.

If you've read this much Bible
    And found Christ for your own,
You'll be so in love with Jesus
    You'll want to read on and on
So read on and on and on!

# O THOU OF LITTLE FAITH

Matthew 14:22-33

I'd like to have been in the ship
    When Jesus came walking on the water,
And see Peter step out of that ship,
    And actually walk on the water.

Jesus said, "O thou of little Faith."
    When Peter began to sink.
If I'd stepped out of that ship
    I'd have had BIG faith, I think.

# WHO'S THE DOUBTER?

Luke 24:36-48

Don't ever blame that Thomas
    Because he had to see.
If I'd seen Christ crucified,
    You'd have to prove it to me.

If I'd seen that dreadful scourge,
    Making His back to bleed,
And having that crown of thorns
    On his brow hit with a reed,

Then having his hands and feet
    Nailed to that wretched cross,
And seeing His precious side
    Pierced, and His blood gush out.

How could I have believed
    That Jesus was alive?
You'd have to prove it to me,
    That He could ever revive.

Don't forget that He already
    Had appeared unto the ten,
And had an awful time
    Proving to those doubting men.

To prove He wasn't a spirit,
    He showed His hands and feet.
They still refused to believe,
    So He took fish and honeycomb to eat.

John 20:24-28
To prove Himself to Thomas,
    Was an easy job.
One glimpse and he exclaimed,
    "My Lord and my God!"

Calling Thomas the Doubter,
    Isn't really fair.
We would probably have doubted,
    If you and I'd been there.

# REUNION

John 11:1-46; 1 Thessalonians 4:13-18

Lazarus was a dear friend of Jesus.
  He enjoyed being with him always.
But Lazarus took sick and died.
  In fact, he had been dead four days.

When Jesus said, "Lazarus, come forth,"
  He came forth all bound in grave clothes.
I wish I could have seen his sisters!
  What a reunion he had with those!

There's going to be another reunion,
  And I'm going to be there this time,
When Jesus calls all those who love Him.
  This time the joy will be mine!

# LISTENING IN

Luke 24:13-48

It would have been so exciting,
    If I could have been listening in,
To the two on the road to Emmaus,
    When Jesus joined them—and then,

Have him sit right down at the table,
    Give thanks, and break bread for them,
As he did when he fed five thousand,
    Then see them recognize Him!

The two rushed back from Emmaus,
    With their story of Jesus alive!
But the ten did not believe them.
    But soon after they arrived,

I wish I could have seen Him appear,
    Through locked doors! What a surprise!
Jesus, right back there with them!
    They could not believe their eyes.

To prove that He was Himself,
    He said, "See my hands and my feet."
They still, "believed not and wondered."
    Before them, he had to eat.

It's so easy for us to believe.
    But if we had been there that day,
We might have been just as unbelieving.
    Praise God! We know Him today!

# HELL

I read over my script,
Before it went to print,
    And worried how often I'd mentioned hell.
I had plenty of poems,
And didn't mind some going.
    I'd just cut them and all would be well.

I thought then, when burnt,
Even a finger, how it hurt,
    And I didn't want anyone to go there.
So I'm leaving them all in,
And trust all to repent of sin,
    Believe and trust Jesus is my prayer.

Heaven's too good to miss.
So tell others all about this,
    And they'll go to heaven as well.
Angels will sing
About the whole thing,
    And we can forget about hell.

CPSIA information can be obtained at www.ICGtesting.com
Printed in the USA
LVOW080604280213

321987LV00002B/71/P